Blockchain Dynamics

*A Quick Beginner's Guide on
Understanding the Foundations of Bitcoin
and Other Cryptocurrencies*

Martin Quest

Table Of Contents

Introduction

You can't fully understand the workings of any cryptocurrency until you understand the blockchain. That is the topic of this book which starts off conceptually – describing the Bitcoin or cryptocurrency that rides on top of it, but slowly and rapidly looking at sufficient detail so that you can get a good foundation in the functional aspect of blockchains.

For those of you who have heard so much (or not at all) about this thing called cryptocurrency, but don't really know what it is, let's start there. A cryptocurrency is a form of currency where you exchange it for goods and services. This exchange of goods and services for a payment of some sort happens online. Happening online does not preclude it from happening in person. We tend to think of them as being mutually exclusive, but, in actual fact, today's technology has made it possible for us to do instant transfers of payment in person using electronic methods and without the need for using cash. Online payments are just as possible when standing face to face with your counterpart, as it is with one sitting in the Arctic, and the other in the Antarctic.

Having sad that, this cryptocurrency is completely independent of any form of central authority and so cross-border transactions are easily accomplished. It takes less than an hour and, in most cases, just 10 minutes to effectively transfer payment from one person to the next. The biggest problem that this kind of system will face, if you think about it, is that there is no enforce of trust. That was the whole point of the trust institutions being erected at the start of civilization. A central authority was needed to make sure that everyone was kept honest and that money would change hands as promised, but the cryptocurrency does away with all that and makes the system trust-neutral. That means we do not need a centralized system to act as the trust institution. We don't need to have anyone print or manage the supply of currency and we do not need any unnecessary printing of currency and waste of paper. Instead, the trust system is kept in what we call a blockchain – which is the topic of this book. We will get to that in more detail shortly, but, for now, we are just getting underway to understand the fundamental overview of cryptocurrencies.

To get a good grasp of the cryptos, we need to think about the role of money. We use bills – paper notes and metal coins, which we call fiat currency, to market the value of the exchange. If you buy a stick of gum at the newsstand, you exchange that stick of gum with a certain value when you hand the cashier a dollar bill. That dollar bill symbolizes the trust institution's guarantee that you will be able to use that same value when you take that dollar bill and give it to someone else for another purchase you make. This means that the dollar bill moves from The Mint when it was first printed, and goes to the bank and to the customer and, from there, it passes hands constantly until its service life is over and it gets sent back to the treasury and is incinerated. When it is incinerated, another bill takes its place. Nothing new is created and nothing old is destroyed; it merely carries the value of one person's labor and contribution.

If you think deeply about it, the ubiquitous paper currency is convenient to use in person, but fails when we can't shred it up and transmit it across broadband to pay for an online purchase. It is more important that we start leaning towards the use of a currency that lends itself to electronic transmission.

There are two things that you need to consider when you come into electronic transmission. The first is that it gives you an opportunity to re-engineer the outdated and expensive trust institutions, and the second is using the centralized systems creates a little bit of a problem as it places too much value in a centralized location. Think about the hacking and theft of online assets. When you put all your assets in one location, any breach will compromise all that. The centralized model, even in data storage, is not that preferred these days.

As an example of the online world and looking to decentralized systems, look at the world of cloud storage. It is increasingly trending towards the use of decentralized and fragmented storage solutions that provide safety and reliability, while protecting against targeted cyber-attacks (i.e. hacking and DDOS attacks) or physical attacks – like property destruction.

In fragmented distributed storage, a single file is broken into smaller pieces, and each piece is then encrypted and sent to multiple locations. There are also duplicates kept at other locations as well. When the user wants to retrieve it, his app pulls all the files from the locations and brings them back and decrypts them. This way, when a server is attacked, the data stays safe.

That is not an example of a blockchain, but the distributed files storage systems use of blockchains to keep track of the data. The example was more to illustrate the value of decentralized systems over centralized ones.

In cryptocurrencies, there is no physical manifestation of value (like the dollar bill); instead, the value is taken from each person's word or promise. It is a messaging system that keeps track of this intent to pay and then transacts that payment. It is called a distributed ledger because it is like a massive ledger with millions of people all paying each other by their word alone, and without a single piece of paper.

That ledger is part of the blockchain and it keeps a record of every transaction in the system, and everyone has total access to that ledger to understand the records if those payments are valid, to confirm ownership of assets, and to facilitate the transfer of value.

The blockchain is the engine that drives all this. On top of the blockchain, everything is just a messaging system. Within the blockchain, the algorithm is sophisticated and, more importantly, the strength of the system is not predicated on the power of the coding, but on the structure of the system. That makes it virtually unhackable from a system's perspective. There are certain security issues but, so far, the system itself has been robust. As we go through the rest of this book, we will discover the genius of the messaging system and the blockchain that supports it underneath. To do this, we will look at the cryptography involved, the common vernacular and definitions of cryptocurrencies and blockchains, the blocks that make up the blockchain, and the proof of work in the mining process.

The bulk of this gives us the full handle we need to form a solid foundation in cryptocurrencies. Remember, the currency is only as robust as the blockchain under it, and the same goes to your understanding of it.

Chapter 1: Fundamentals Of Cryptocurrencies

To understand the ecosystem, and before we reintroduce the concept of messaging intent to transfer value, we will look at the ecosystem of a blockchain and the basis of a coin or token in the world of cryptocurrencies. The definition may seem alien, but it is fairly easy once you get through the basics. The terms are not listed in alphabetical order, but in the order that will best serve you in layering on the understanding of the subject matter.

Nodes

Nodes are a good place to start. They are the points in a network and are typically considered the computer or terminal in each network, but they are actually, and more specifically, the instance of the Application that is running the Bitcoin protocol – which is called Bitcoind. Each node has a particular address and starts off by getting online, then downloading and installing Bitcoind, if you want to be part of the Bitcoin network. Other cryptos have other blockchain versions and instances and have different apps that create this on your computer.

There are approximately 12,000 nodes in the Bitcoin system, and this can be visualized on a map. You can find that here: https://bitnodes.earn.com/. The nodes form the network that is decentralized and each node can talk to another node if it wants to and, over the life of the network, every node would have talked to every other node. This is essentially a P2P network that we will describe next.

There are two kinds of nodes. The first is a lite node and that node just keeps track of the transaction that node has taken part in, and the other is the regular node that keeps track of all the transactions in the entire ecosystem.

P2P

P2P stands for Peer-to-Peer and it is a network that people, through their computers and devices, can become a part of it. P2P initially was popular for its file-sharing features during the days of Napster. The content was deemed an infringement of copyright, but the technology and the concept was quite sound. It just didn't go anywhere until the advent of cryptocurrencies.

There is no need to do any major programming as the app will usually do everything that is necessary. You just have to load it up, install it, and the app will open up a port – typically port 8332. From there, it connects to other nodes in the network and communicates pre-determined information. It doesn't allow anything in the rest of your computer to be seen or shared. The P2P format is just for a way for individual computers to come together and become a network without any centralized server. In the typical internet infrastructure, there is a client-server relationship. All the data sits in the server, and the client engage the server and ask for the information. The information is centralized and, if in the event of a hack, a DDOS (Distributed Denial of Service) attack that disables the server, or even physical acts of terrorism on the server farm, all will be lost. In the distributed system, an attack cannot disable the entire system because each node is not dependent on the other node. If one node goes down, there are still numerous nodes left to fill the gap in any way. In the Bitcoin ecosystem, the nodes broadcast information to each other. It is the way to spread information across the network. If one node gets hacked or DDOS'd, the other nodes can still provide reliable copies of the information. The advantages of a P2P network versus a centralized server architecture can be appreciated, especially in blockchains. When you add blockchains to a P2P network, you get a system that is robust and impenetrable, yet easily deployable across a global landscape.

Ledger

A ledger only seems to invoke the notion of a great big book that stores all the information of each person's account, its current balance and the transactions relevant to that account. If that is your notion then, you are almost 100% correct. The ledger is an electronic record of all transaction, from the transaction of the very first coin, to the very last transaction. Every single one of those transactions can be traced back to the very beginning, and those transactions can be mapped.

So, in essence, this ledger is a live document and the updates are transmitted across the node that keeps a copy of their ledger on the computer that hosts the app. That ledger has grown to a fairly large file at this point. Each time a person starts up a new node, they typically have to download the entire ledger from the first transaction all the way to the most recent, and then keep its ears open to update the ledger as and when a transaction is complete.

The value of this distributed ledger is priceless and inexpensive. Each person who is a member of the network, and who uses the network, bears the cost of his own computer and it is incidental to his own use of the computer, so the cost of the distributed system becomes fragmented and inconsequential. This is the first benefit of such a system. As opposed to the public cost of maintaining a centralized infrastructure to print, regulate, enforce and defend the currency, cryptos are relatively uncomplicated and market-driven.

The node's responsibility goes more than just maintaining the ledger, it is also tasked with reviewing the transaction that is transmitted to it, and to figure out if an address has the funds it needs to spend it, or not spend it twice.

Gossip Protocol

The nodes in the network communicate on an algorithm with the Bitcoind called the gossip protocol. When a block is completed, that block needs to be transmitted to the ledgers contained in each node, and that block has a certain identification number. One node will ask another node if it has that block, and if that node doesn't, then it will transfer that block for this new node to save. That node will then randomly select another block and find out if that node has the new information. It also does another thing. Once it has told the node its information, it asks that node if it has other new information and compares it to what it already has. If the information from the other node is not within its ledger, then it will take that information as well. That way there is a two-way exchange of information.

Each node contacts six other nodes (in most cases that is true, but you can adjust your Bitcoind app to contact more nodes if you like). In most cases, nodes just contact six others at random. The node they choose is randomly selected and so, each time it opens a communication to a node, it is a different set of nodes. This keeps the system safe by not allowing predictability of who the node contacts are.

If each contact six, then theoretically, it will only take six hops from any new piece of information originating from a node to reach all existing nodes. Think about it like this – the first node passes it to six nodes and each of them pass it to six more. That makes 36 nodes that are now up-to-date on that information which was broadcast by the first node. Those 36 then broadcast to six more which makes it 216. That's three jumps so far. From there, it becomes 1,296, and then 7,776 on the fifth hop. On the sixth hop, it becomes 46,656, but there are only 12,000 nodes at this point which means that it only takes a little over five hops to disseminate all the information of every transaction to the entire ecosystem. That happens in just a few seconds and everyone is up-to-date. The gossip protocol is extremely effective and can be used in larger ecosystems effectively.

Consensus Methods

This consensus algorithm is a feature contained with the blockchain's algorithm. It is a core function in that it keeps the system in check and avoids the forking of the blockchain. It can be said that the consensus algorithm is related to the gossip protocol because it tells the next node what it knows, and also checks to see if that node has anything to add. It tries to build a consensus of what is right and what is not. An occasion that requires the execution of the consensus protocol hardly happens, but if it does, the protocol staves of a forking in the chain.

The consensus algorithm takes information from the node population, attaching it to the previous block that it has in its version of memory. In the event that someone tries to make their own block (or alter a block to include an unsanctioned transaction), the few nodes around the offending node may accept the block for a few moments. The moment they receive word of the other block that has really been accepted by the general network population, and that information gets to them, they will now realize that there are two blocks in the system vying for the same space in the chain.

Because two blocks can't occupy the same spot in the chain, the nodes that receive conflicting information will await the next confirmation. They will then look at the block that was used, and they will also use that block. Eventually, the block that has the longest chain survives.

For any block to be confirmed, it has to have the consensus of 50% + 1 of the nodes in the network. The only way the node in the network will accept the newly minted block is if it is part of the longest chain. That is the only way the nodes (or rather the algorithm in the nodes) will reach a consensus. If there is a discrepancy as we mentioned earlier, then the nodes will wait until the next block is attached and then the next block, and then the next one, until it starts to see the pattern of blocks that are slowly increasing. It will then erase from its memory the offending block. The entire network will reflect the appropriate transactions in the block at that point.

This is why you should wait for at least three confirmations to ship your product. It is not until there are a few confirmations built on top of the block that contains your transaction that you can be confident that the payment is legitimate.

Messages

A transaction is when Mr. A sends Mr. B a message saying that he is sending him 1BTC. Remember that's all it takes because it is a message. Once the message is sent, the system materializes the intention of the sender. The first thing the node does is check if the sender has the right to spend that 1BTC. Basically, it checks to see if the balance is sufficient to cover the intended amount to be sent over. If the amount is sufficient, then the node conducts 16 points of verification that is found in the logarithm and, if that all checks out, then the node broadcasts that transaction.

These are the list of checks that it conducts:

- Each transaction, which is a message, must be less than the maximum block size of 1 MB.

- Transaction sizes must be greater than, or equal to 100 bytes.

- The value of each transaction must not be less than 0 and not more than 21 million BTC.

- There can be no hash inputs that are equal to 0.

- The complete data structure is correct.

- The locking script must match the standard format.

- The lock time must be less than the maximum allowed number.

- The number of signatures must be less than the signature limit.

- Unlocking script can only push numbers onto the stack.

- With each input, the output must exist and not have been spent.

- All input and outputs must have values.

- The full transaction's syntax must be correct.

But that transaction doesn't go to the rest of the nodes. It is then placed in a queue and sent to what are called miners. Miners need to take this transaction after the node verifies it and place it in what is called a block. We will look at what a block is a little farther down. In most cases, once the transaction is done, it is considered complete, but it is always best to wait for confirmation that the payment is complete. Confirmation is done by the mining process. Mining is done by miners and is described in the chapter on Mining.

Account Balance

The account balance that you see in the software does not have some kind of recording of the amount you send and receive, meaning it doesn't record your activities while you send and receive. Instead, it looks at the blockchain to get the data it needs. The wallet scours the blockchain for every transaction that that address was a part of. If there were no transactions, then the account balance would show zero. The point of this is that you can log on to any Bitcoind node and enter the address you are looking for and it will always show you the current balance in that account. You don't even need a Bitcoind app for that; in fact, you can even go to the Bitcoin website and look up an address and you would see the available balance and the transaction history of that account. When you open up your wallet, you would have to enter the address you are interested in messaging from, or accepting funds and look at the balance. If you want to move that balance, then you would have to provide the private key and move it from there.

Genesis Block and New Coins

Most of you would have heard of this thing called the Genesis Block. As you can imagine, it is the block that first started out and it was the block that transactions from the coins that the developer awarded himself. Since there was nothing to mine at the time and the coins had to come first, the initial transactions were done by the developer, and when he mined those blocks, he got more coins. It started from there and, eventually, as more people caught on, more miners were needed to put the transactions in blocks. You will see how this works in the Mining chapter.

New coins are added to the network every ten minutes, or thereabouts. The exact time is not fixed, but it is fairly accurate. The reason is that the coins are not released randomly. The miners have to solve a puzzle in order to get the reward – that reward is in the form of new coins. The miner then sells those coins and gets whatever he agrees for in return. In most cases, the miners go to the exchange markets and exchange them for fiats because their mining equipment and computational power and energy usages are paid in hard currency. That does two things. First, it allows new participants to come in because there is always a seller among the miners, and new entrants have a way to get new coins. The second is that it increases the supply of coins in a predictable way. That keeps the inflation of BTC at a predictable and falling rate over time. The maximum number of coins that will ever be released is 21,000,000 and that amount will be reached in the next few years.

There are no other ways of creating new coins and, once the system reaches its limit, those are all the coins that can be in the market.

To avoid a supply problem, you have to realize that the coins are not limited by their denomination. Each Bitcoin can be divided into 100,000,000 (one hundred million) parts. Each part is called a Satoshi. In the event that the limit is reached and the coins are so successful and prevalent that a million more users come on board, then the market price will adjust in a certain way that it would be common place to transact in Satoshis than it would be to transact in Bitcoins.

It is a reverse inflation question that is resolved by the management of the denomination. For instance, you now pay about 10,000 USD for 1 BTC. For some people, that's more than they need and they just want to buy a little at a time to pay for the ISP service – for instance. That ISP is charging $10, payable in BTC, which would be 0.001 BTC. If I purchased 1 BTC for this, it would last me 1,000 months. So, what's the point? Instead, I can buy 100,000 Satoshis or 0.001 BTC for $10 and use that to pay my ISP, but that example is not to tell you to pay your ISP with BTC; no, it is about showing you that you can break a BTC into its smallest component. When you do that when the supply of BTC stops, the fiat value of something can be expressed in Satoshis rather than in BTC, so, instead of having only twenty one million units of BTC to work with, you can have 2.1 trillion Satoshis. That would be enough to supply the world for some time to come.

Chapter 2: Cryptography

There is a significant amount of mathematics that goes into the entire Bitcoin ecosystem - from hashing, to cryptography, and even probability, and that is then merged with the powers of computing. The outcomes are a structurally-secure platform that can handle the demands of a robust online currency and still be run semi-autonomously without the need for central authorities, and yet be trust-neutral.

To understand the power of the blockchain better, it is best that we dive in headfirst into the cryptography that drives the whole thing. After all, that is what it is called crypto – for cryptography.

Hashes, Hashing and SHA 256

To understand the cryptography, the first thing we need to look at is the SHA 256. This is a 256 bit Secure Hashing Algorithm. Without getting too much in the way the algorithm works, you can easily go to an online hashing website and enter whatever you want and get the hash for it.

Try it.

Go to https://passwordsgenerator.net/sha256-hash-generator/

Place this sentence in the box: The Cow Jumped Over The Moon

In return, you will get this:

3474A5E82F8FED7D5C9FBDC181ED562815C7C95F2D0C6B2D10C502ECB2A39043

Now, place the same sentence, but just alter the first alphabet and change it to lower case, like this:

the Cow Jumped Over The Moon

Note that only the first alphabet has changed, and even then by only altering the case and, when the sentence is put into the box and hashed, this is the outcome:

E7EEA2B7CE4F32A53337A15D85F5F2B5A6A8E65CEE6283117C8432C58FF68E70

For such a small difference in the change of the original sentence, the change in the output is starkly different. This is one of the reasons you cannot reverse engineer the original phrase; hence, it makes it a secure hashing algorithm.

If you haven't guessed it, hashing just means to change any sentence and put it into the seemingly random character string. Here is another example. If you take the entire Introduction chapter from this book, which is over a thousand words, it gives us this:

```
821EA5FEFA1E48DE85E30E13378A616CECD188D2CD609A2B315472ED4C474DFA
```

It still gives us a similarly-looking string of characters, but you will never be able to reverse engineer this string to return to the content of the Introduction by just the hash. This makes it extremely secure.

Private Keys

The key to the entire thing as far as a user is concerned is the secrecy of his private key. Users have private keys that can authorize payments when one sends a message from an address. The private key is the core of everything. If you lose your private key to the address, then you should transfer your money out and get a new address. The secrecy of the key is of paramount importance.

Private keys are generated first. It is a random number that is chosen from a robust random number generator between 1 and 2^{97}. It is impossible to guess any number, or to end up using it more than once. To be able to guess that number will take more energy than there is in our sun, so the number is fairly secure.

Once a random number generator gets this number, it can then be converted to a public key and that public key is then converted to an address. Now that you know that the hash only works one way, you will also know that the Bitcoin address that is given to anyone to send the message to the money cannot be reverse engineered. This is the way the private keys are kept secure and this is the way that the entire Bitcoin infrastructure is managed.

Just for fun, if you take a simple number, your birthday perhaps, and take a hash of that, so let's say your date of birth is 1.1.1911, so you put in 01011911 in the hash generator, this is what you get:

```
FA372F9E71529403A63AFFB4E5C04E466E63D567CB054F1CBFCFD5B7FCD36E50
```

Now, imagine that is the string you want to use as your private key. To convert that to your public key, it requires another mathematical operation. We will look at this in the next section.

Public Keys

With the private key in hand, you can now generate the corresponding public key. To generate the public key, there is an asymmetric mathematical function that takes one number (the private key) and plots it on an elliptic curve then generates the public key from the resulting line that intersects the curve. So, in essence, the public key is derived from the private key, but you cannot reverse engineer the private key from the public key. You must always keep the private key confidential and, if possible, try not to keep it on your computer in case it is hacked or has catastrophic failure. If you can, place it in a cold wallet – something that does not connect to the Internet. Use it only when you need to spend the money in a particular address.

Bitcoin Address

Your Bitcoin address is where someone who is paying you sends you the transaction message, but, remember, this is not a bank account, but more like an email address. They are merely sending you a message. Inside that message, you can write anything you want in addition to the message that specifically includes an amount of the funds to be transferred. Remember the other nodes will check this. If there is insufficient value to transfer, then the message will not be included in the block or unsuccessful.

This Bitcoin address is mathematically linked to both the public key and the private key, by extension. It is merely the SHA256 hash of the public key.

So, now what you have are three numbers that constitute the core of the Bitcoin network as it pertains to you, the sender, or to you as the receiver.

You use the Bitcoin address to send and receive funds, you then use the public key to show that you have the right to send the message from the address and you use the private key as the password to prove to the system that you indeed have the authority to manage the account and dispatch the message.

To put it simply, when you put in your private key, the app automatically looks to see if it corresponds to the public key. If it does, then your message will be authentic and that would result in the message being permitted to pass through the network.

The five things that you need to prepare you for the upcoming blockchain overview is the hashing algorithm used in all things related to Bitcoin – the SHA256; you then need to understand how private keys are generated and what you need to do to keep yourself secure so that no one can guess them and no one can brute force them. You then need to understand the role of public keys and how Bitcoin addresses are generated. You have all that. With that, you can now go on to the next layer of the issue which are blocks and transactions.

Chapter 3: Blocks and Transactions

Before we get into miners and mining, we need to make a quick stop at trying to understand blocks and transactions. It is important to know and understand that Bitcoin transactions are not typical remittances that we think of, but rather they are messages of an indication to give someone (the recipient) the value (in Bitcoin) that you (the sender) already possess. I repeat this often in this book because there is a large body of misunderstood and ill-described material out in the ether. Many people still think that cryptocurrency is a physical coin because they see these images online that show a conventional coin embossed with the Bitcoin logo and the circuit board etching and think it is some form of an electric coin. None of this is true and you have to really understand the concept of the message and the transactions that is driven by it.

It is the ultimate contract where man's word is literally his value – when the message is sent – it is as good as gold. That's the point of Bitcoin.

Ok, so we already know that transactions are messages that go from sender to receiver and that message transfers a certain amount that the sender has to the receiver's address. But where does that value come from? How does it get injected into the electronic network and the Bitcoin network in particular?

Your currency should be convenient for your habits of exchange. If you go to the marketplace in the town's square, then carrying wads of cash fifty years ago was appropriate. Today, the town square has become the global square and the marketplace has become accessible via the Internet but the value carriers only lend themselves to physical exchanges.

But where does the sender get it from? Well, the sender has only three ways of having a coin in his address. He either mined it, bought it, or someone paid him for a product or service. He cannot just create it out of thin air – and that is an important point to make for two reasons. First, for those of you who are thinking that you could just make a string of numbers up, you can't, and I will explain why in a moment. Second, you can't just spend it twice either – well, that is another way of making your own coin, and you can't do that either. The system is very adept at preventing that from happening and it's not just the code that is in the system but the fact that it is a distributed system. I am a pentester, and I have tried, as an exercise, to penetrate the Bitcoin nodes in my basement from a remote computer. I can't ever seem to break the system, and that is a good thing for many reasons. It means that the only weak link in the whole chain is the person holding the private key. In that way, it is like pasting your ATM pin number on your card so you won't forget it. If you can keep your private key safe, you are not going to lose your coins.

This brings us back to creating coins out of thin air – you can't. The whole purpose of the blocks in the blockchain, and the mining that is required, is threefold:

1. To allow miners to expend something of value in the real world so that something of value can be created in the electronic world.

2. To give each coin or token legitimacy by giving it the credibility of past use. The more it is used, the more subsequent users know that that coin has the ability to be a legitimate carrier of value – that chain of blocks replaces the centralized need for a trust institution to legitimize the carrier of value the way governments do for paper currency.

3. Finally, it precludes forgery so that not one, but every participant is able to validate and store the credibility and legitimacy of the coin. This obviates the need, again, for a centralized system.

To get a more internalized understanding of this, it would serve you well to look at the philosophical and historical evolution of the mechanisms of exchange. We can't go through the full details and full history of the evolution of money, but we will do the best we can to give the current issue context.

Philosophy of Equity and Exchange

This is the crux of the whole Bitcoin value transfer system and this is where you need to disengage your mind from what you and I are so used to. We are used to the printed piece of paper with Jackson, Franklin and Washington printed on them to be something of value on its own. We forget that fiat currency only represents a value. It is in paper form because it's a lot easier to fold and put in your money clip or wallet. That makes it easy to carry around. Imagine having to carry around a cart full of gold to make your transactions. That dollar bill merely carries the value of something that you did in the past to get it that value. You may have labored at the office, or profited at your business, and your contribution of value resulted in the conversion of that dollar. That dollar on its own is a piece of paper. It has value because you worked for it and the sovereign government of the land you live in has printed these (supposedly) unforgeable mediums of exchange as a public good.

That fiat currency – the dollar bill, or gold coin, is just a vessel of value. The actual value itself is not that thing that carries it. You went to work, got paid, took that money and bought bread. Money served as the medium of value that could easily move between getting paid by your employer, to being used as the medium to purchase products so that it made transactions more convenient. Otherwise, you would have to go to the baker and barter him with your skill to get a loaf of bread – what a headache.

So, what we have established painstakingly is that value is different from its carrier. Now that we know that, then we can willingly make the carrier more relevant to the venue and method of interaction. We used physical paper when we traded physically. Now we trade electronically, so something electronic is appropriate. We already mentioned this part and you get that, but here is the point of all this. You see, printed fiats have one thing going for them and that is that the government that printed them places their weight behind the piece of paper and says that they stand behind it – and that gives the people the assurances that they need that the paper can hold the value that the people put in it.

Make no mistake, the value of the currency does not come from the institutions of trust that the government represents, the value comes from the labor and contribution that people put in to it; whereas, once the government provided security for it, they also ended up giving it value because the fiat was backed by the total output of the country and managed by the supply of the printed bill. In cryptocurrencies, none of that exists and so the only way you can give the currency value and give it credibility and give people the confidence to use it is if it has a track record. By that, I don't just mean that Bitcoin in general and as a whole needs to get credibility, I mean the value and utility of each Satoshi and Bitcoin needs to have the credibility. In fact, to make it plausible and serve as a carrier, that carrier must have a credible starting point and usage over time to develop a history of its use. Without that history, and without that credible starting point, that coin has no value since it does not have the backing of a sovereign body.

I know it's been a pretty philosophical and long trip to get from the start of this discussion to this point – but it is necessary to describe the weight of the blockchain. You would be remiss to undervalue the prominence of the blockchain in the future of human interaction, and it would be easy to dismiss it if you did not understand the philosophical aspect of the blockchain.

Because human exchange is about the exchange of value, and value can only be created by expenditure of effort, it would be impossible to transition from the physical world to the electronic one without the correct procedure and without effort.

Transactions

As I mentioned, each transaction transfers a certain amount of coin from a person who has it, to a person who is about to receive it. A person without a coin in their account can't send any, but a person with a fresh, brand new address can receive any amount. There are no limitations to creating as many addresses as possible. Remember, the number of addresses you can open is equivalent to the number of private keys you can generate. There are 2^{97} possible private keys that you can generate and while that may look small, here is what that actually looks like:

1.5845633 x 10^{29} - to make that more evident – that's:

158,456,330,000,000,000,000,000,000,000.

To put that into perspective, earth has 7.5 x 10^{15} grains of sand. That means if each grain of sand was an earth-like planet that had the same number of grains of sand contained within it, then the number of private keys you could generate would all the grains of sand combined. Get it... ok, it's a lot. Trust me on that one.

The reason we take the trouble to make it a point to stress this is that the chance of a collision is remote, in statistical terms, and this just means that if you keep the pick of your private key perfectly random, the chances of you finding a private key that hasn't been taken yet is very close to zero.

Those odds dramatically change if you pick a number that you like – your birthday for instance, or your anniversary and then try to convert that to a hash and then use that to create the public key and a Bitcoin address; what you will find is that it's probably already taken. The collision rate goes up significantly the moment you do not let the private key be randomly picked by a truly random number generator. You can find one here: https://www.random.org/strings/

Once you pick a random number, you can write that number down somewhere and then, my suggestion is that you run it through a SHA256 convertor like we did earlier and that will give you the hash of that number. You can then take that as your private key and generate the public key from there and then get a Bitcoin address from there.

All that is comparatively a lot of work, because if you have a Bitcoind on your computer, it is going to generate an account, and a public and private key for you as many times as you want. By the way, you can download that here: https://bitcoin.org/en/download. It will be as easy as pie and you should just stick to doing it that way. I have mentioned the process so you understand how it's done and that will give you an understanding of how the blockchain works as well under it.

Now that we took that minor detour, let's get back to our topic of transactions. When you conduct a transaction, it is a message telling the world that you, Mr. A, are sending Mr. B, X BTC. Remember, you are not just telling Mr. B, so be careful of the text message that you include in the message. Once you send that message to the world, all nodes are listening. Remember the gossip protocol as it starts to work at this point and the message gets into the queue and the nodes go into action to verify that your message can be a message. Assuming all goes well, the transaction is righteous and it gets confirmed and the recipient is now the legal owner of the coin.

The coin takes on life because of transactions, and the transactions have value because of the coin. There are two aspects of value when it comes to a coin. The first is that no coin comes free – putting aside the initial coins that were released to the developer to get the ball rolling, but, even then, one could convincingly argue that the coins were reward for the sweat equity that was put into the development of the protocol and the algorithm that was built on top of it.

From the very first transaction until today, every coin starts its life with a certain intrinsic value. That value is defined as the value that miners put in to do the computation necessary to create the block. Why we need the block, and how that is important, we will talk about in this chapter, but in the next section.

The second part of the value that can be assigned to the coin is the value of net demand. If net demand is positive, then the intrinsic value that the coins have will gain a premium. If the net demand is negative, then the coins will erode from their intrinsic value and eventually grind to a halt and be worth nothing.

As with anything in commerce, the value of one thing can exist in a vacuum, but to know and transmit that value, it has to be expressed in terms of another commodity or item of value. In the case of Bitcoin and other cryptocurrency, there is a vibrant exchange market that gives you an accurate determination of value in almost any other fiat currency of value. In US dollar terms, the value of BTC (Bitcoin)has risen from mere pennies per BTC to $5, then on to $50 and on to $500, and all the way up to almost $20,000. Yes, that was twenty-thousand dollars. It wasn't a typo.

Old school economists can't fathom why something that has no tangible link – like how the dollar is linked to the sovereign wealth of a country, can end up being worth so much. The reason is not because it is a secret currency or that it has some nefarious advantage; what they don't get is that it is the appropriate innovation for the colliding of two socio-economic phenomena – online commerce, and distrust of centralized authority.

The value of the Bitcoin has been defined by the Fiat currency put in the physical world. Some people think that that makes BTC untenable as a major currency in the future, but that doesn't matter, because Bitcoin in itself is not designed to displace sovereign currency.

The things to remember about transactions are this:

1. Transactions are messages that are broadcast to the entire network and are carried across the nodes by the gossip protocol.

2. All transactions are irreversible, so don't make a mistake.

3. Each transaction is automatically given an irrevocable transaction ID, regardless of size. A transaction ID looks like this (example): 447acbdb6a6c42d438617e5a6785d342d5a96a0a01500a65b7a93127e18f9a0a If you click on it, it will take you to the blockchain.org and give you the information of that transaction.

4. Each TXID (transaction ID) will list out the address that sent the payment and the address that received it. Details about TXIDs are presented next.

Transaction ID

That transaction ID is then placed in a pool - assuming that the nodes have considered the transaction to be legit. Once the transaction is in a pool, all the transaction IDs plus the header information (typical things like date and time stamp, block number and something called a nonce) is placed in the block and hashed.

Hashes and hashing were described and discussed in Chapter 2. Once they are hashed, the block returns a unique string of alphanumeric characters. You saw within that section that even the smallest change, like altering one character in the entire text by changing it from a lower case to an upper case, renders the hash absolutely and unmistakably different and thus changes to it can't be made if you do not want to disrupt all that is built around it. Even if a person were to hack a system and sneak in a transaction retroactively, the hash wouldn't match and the nonce wouldn't work and the block will fail but, if somehow a malicious actor was determined enough to mine the block and get the proper nonce for the block, the problem is the hash for the original block was placed in the subsequent block and hashed out. Remember that each block includes the hash of the last block among other things so if you want to alter a transaction six blocks deep, then when you go to hash that block, the hash that is supposed to appear in the next block will change, and that alters the next block. If you want to go ahead and alter that block as well, you would have to put in a huge amount of hashing power just to get one transaction changed. After two to three blocks, the benefit becomes unworthy of the effort.

But mining is not so simple because within the transaction IDs, time and date stamp and previous block number, there is that thing we call nonce. Remember that? Well, the nonce is a really a random number, and that random number is used to control the resulting hash.

Why does the system need to control the outcome of that hash? They do that so that there are opportunities for the miners to do the puzzle that process the hashes until it gets the format it is looking for. The first miner to get the hash gets the reward. Once the block is hashed, it is placed in sequence and the next block is processed and it will include the block hash of the previous block.

Do you see the genius of the system?

Blocks

Ok, so this is where it gets interesting. If you have been looking deeply at transactions, you must be considering how on earth you pass on the value of something without it being subjected to forgery and manipulation. Well, that's what blocks are for.

Each transaction is about 100 kb in size and can vary upwards from there, as long as it is not over the 1 MB limit. As multiple transactions are accumulated, the nodes shuttle them into a queue so that a miner can take them and lock them up in blocks.

This is where it gets confusing for most people, so pay attention.

A group of transactions is called a block, but it does not stop there. These transactions are accumulated and if you look at this block, for instance, block number 520763, you can see in blockchain.info when you search for blocks by number, it will tell you all the transactions that are listed by TXID.

When a block is constructed, it is done so by the miners and that will be discussed a little more in that chapter. When the miners put it together, they typically take them as they are, but it is not uncommon for miners to choose which transactions they want to include and which they do not. There is an incentive for them by choosing the ones that have the highest fees. You see Bitcoin has a standard fee, but senders are more than welcome to increase the amount they are paying to expedite the confirmation times. So depending on this amount, the miners would prioritize the transactions and load them up into a block, and then they get started with the puzzle-solving which is to mine the block. You will see that part in the mining chapter.

Once these blocks are mined, they will be given a block number and they will be layered sequentially. Each block has its own unique composition and unique transaction ID sets. They will never be duplicated and no transaction is part of more than one block. Each block is then stitched mathematically to the block that preceded it and the subsequent block will be stitched mathematically to this present block.

We will show you all of this in the mining chapter.

But the point to make here is that because the TXIDs are unique for every transaction, the number just can't be used again, and the fact that the number will never be repeated makes it impossible for anyone to alter the transaction by using the same transaction ID. If you add to that, that once the TXID is placed in a block, and the block is tied to the previous block, then it is impossible to undo anything that happened in the last block because that would alter all the subsequent blocks after that.

Blocks give individual transactions the credibility of existence and confidence of usability. It obviously works because the market price has been consistently above $5000 per Bitcoin – more than the price of gold. Check out the historic price of Bitcoin here: https://charts.bitcoin.com/chart/price#cat-market

We call it a coin to make it easier to explain, but you have seen there really isn't a coin physically present and here is how I can illustrate that to you. You know that 1 BTC can be divided up into 100,000,000 Satoshis. That means if I sell my car to a friend and he pays me 1 BTC for it, I now have 1 BTC in my account. I can then send out 1,000 Satoshis to someone for mowing my lawn, or 1,000,000 Satoshis to my ISP and still have a balance of 98,999,000. If it was physical, how did I just break it up? Ok, so it's not physical.

Now that we understand the nature of blocks, we will see what is in it, how it is formed and how it is stitched together in the next chapter.

In wrapping up this chapter, we have just begun to understand a major component of the blockchain and thereby understand the mechanism under the hood of cryptocurrencies like Bitcoin.

Chapter 4: Miners and Mining

Miners do the mining, so if you know what mining is then you know what miners do. So what is mining? No, it is not taking a pickaxe and chipping away at a cave wall to expose the precious metal in the stone.

Mining is a computational and mathematical process that places these blocks we've talked about in previous chapters in a sequence that cannot be retroactively altered. Once the transaction is in the block, a confirmation is said to be complete. That takes about ten minutes. If you really want the transaction to be solid, in the event it is a large transaction, then wait for six confirmations and you can be dead certain that the transaction is confirmed and without any possibility that the sender will reverse the transaction.

How does this work?

While regular nodes are in charge of going through a checklist and making sure every transaction that is broadcast to them from a neighbor passes all the time on the checklist, the miner is responsible for something just as important. The miner has to legitimize the blocks and tie them together to the preceding block.

This takes a large investment and a tremendous effort and is not as simple as one may think based on the description earlier in this book. In the rest of this chapter, we will go through the other processes and show you how difficult, expressive and how it requires a high level of skill to execute.

To act as a barrier, the Bitcoin system requires that only able parties are invoked in the mining operations of putting together blocks. What is even more brilliant about this system is that the difficulty and complexity scaled up with interest. When Bitcoins first entered the market, almost anyone who wanted to be a miner could – they just needed a regular old PC to do it and they could start mining but, as more and more people got clued on to Bitcoin and wanted to mine, the processing requirements evolved.

It now takes expensive equipment, and lots of it, to be able to make a return on your effort. There are not mining farms as large as factories and this has precluded the individual from using spare resources on his laptop to participate.

Just keep this at the back of your mind as we start explaining the proof of work and why it's needed and then we will expand from there to the complexity of the mining process and how that is determined.

Proof of Work

To put it simply (and we will explain this here in greater detail) your Proof of Work

(POW) is the way the system knows that effort has gone into creating the block. This is how it knows that the lock was not just thrown together and that resources of value had to be expended in terms of time, energy and assets that had to be deployed to do the work that comes up with the solution.

The proof of doing the work is contained in the solution to the puzzle. You can guess at it, or you can approach it from a particular direction; you can come at it in any way you want, but the point is that you have to work at it and keep trying until you get it. When you do, and if you are the first one to solve the puzzle, then you get to submit that block as the next in the chain and get your reward for that.

The miner first chooses the transaction he wants to place in the block, and then starts to conduct a hashing operation on it. The transaction IDs are placed in a Merkle Root and the rest of the information is added. This, as you saw, includes the time, date, previous block's hash and the nonce.

This is where the puzzle comes in.

Puzzle

The puzzle is to solve the nonce. Let me show you how. Imagine that the information that was to enter the block included the following items, and let me just use random information to mimic a real block.

Received Time   2018-05-02 00:01:47

Miner

SlushTool

Previous Block Hash
        00000000000000000003169d3297051de41502f769f2c36f6abffa7db8985ba77

Merkle Root

57c16f1ab60394b5de123835f4f4beaafbc9629429292b0cb238fc228f798f70

If you were to hash the above information, you would get this:

EB603B946FDA9F623C2D8770B60DA775AD7B99EAC082B319116BA39664A6D04E

If you notice, the nonce is not present in the information above, and it is not in the hash result. Now, just to prove a point, I am going to just say that the nonce is 1 and so I am going to add the number 1 to the whole thing and run the hash program again. This is what I get:

E8B3CB25EA9D72236999330B7D2AFA878FDE9AA35D16A6EF42F52D4024972247

You see the hash has changed.

If I change the nonce to 2, this is what I get:

4A03F84264FADC60A1A9A6BD90C1B1DD3033590C7844DED0166379332559AB83

So, you get the point – changing the nonce alters the hash output. What if my constraint was that I want the output hash to be something that starts with the number 0? What do I do then? Well, since I cannot reverse engineer it, I am left with only one way of solving that constraint, and that is to randomly look for numbers that would get me that nonce.

So, let's say we use this constraint as an example – I want to have the hash start with zero. That means I have to keep randomly guessing the nonce until I find the nonce that results in the hash starting with zero. For this example, I had to randomly try it until I found that the nonce of 222128 resulted in the hash being:

0522BF5F28591F9F6D190EEDACFC700B869D3C35EF3DEF5023D57029589AE448

So, this hash satisfies the condition that the hash has to start with the number 0.

It was fairly simple and it took me a few minutes of repeated calculations to get the nonce I needed, but this was a simple constraint. The typical constraint is significantly higher in complexity and difficulty.

You can see it in two ways. First off, you can see the hash of the last block which is included in the current block. It is:

000000000000000000003169d3297051de41502f769f2c36f6abffa7db8985ba77

If you notice the hash has 18 zeros up front. That means the algorithm assigned the miner the puzzle and told him he needed to find the nonce that would result in a hash that began with 18 zeros.

That is not always the case. The system alters the number of zeros it wants the miner to find based on the difficulty it deems appropriate. One zero is fairly easy to obtain, two zeros in sequential order would be less so, and, by the time you get to 10 or 18 zeros, you would have to hash millions of times before you can get to the answer that you are looking at. However, the many zeros the system is going to constrain you with depends on what it deems the difficulty should be for you to be able to find the nonce. The level of difficulty that is needed can be ascertained at any point by looking at the difficulty chart info here: https://blockchain.info/charts/difficulty

To better understand this difficulty measure and place it in context, we need to look at the hash rate and get an understanding of that as well. This brings us to hash rates and mining rigs.

Hash Rate

The current hash rate can be found here: https://blockchain.info/charts/hash-rate. It indicates that the rate has been rising steadily over time and that it currently stands at approximately 31 million terahashes per second (TH/s). That is an extremely high number because 1 terahash already means 10^{12} or 1,000,000,000,000, or one trillion hashes. Can you imagine the computational power that needs to go into computing 1 trillion hashes per second? Now, imagine that multiplied by 30 million. That's the level of hashing that is going on now in the mining world for Bitcoin to keep the currency going.

Every second that goes by, all the miners in the world are collectively calculating 31,000,000,000,000,000,000 – thirty one million trillion hashes every second. The more miners that come online, the more that difficulty number is going to go up. Miners enter the fray to be the first to solve the puzzle and claim the reward which is 12.5 Bitcoins at the moment. In one day, 12.5 Bitcoins are released every ten minutes. That means 75 Bitcoins an hour are up for grabs. At today's market value of almost 10,000 dollars, that's 750,000 a day that can be gained from mining. This is the reason you see miners flood the market because there are significant amounts of revenue up for grabs.

But the system is built in such a way that the more hash power there is, the more difficult the puzzle. This is because the intention of the developers of Bitcoin was to have a predictable interval between the release of new Bitcoins into the population. Remember Bitcoin is released only through miners as a reward for their mining contribution. To keep this consistently at ten minutes (or close to it), the system monitors the hash rate that is online, plus the timing it took the last few puzzles to be solved. You can see that here: https://bitinfocharts.com/comparison/bitcoin-confirmationtime.html

If the system sees that there are so many miners and the hash rate increases to the point that they are finding solutions faster than 9 minutes or less, then the system changes the nonce constraint and may say we now need there to be 19 zeros and that will add a few more minutes of processing time.

Mining Rig

This is a good time to start talking about mining rigs and how the Bitcoin blockchain is kept alive. While we are on the subject, you should come to realize by now that in the event that there are no more miners, then the entire system comes to a halt because the blocks will stop being attached to the chains.

Miners are categorized in two ways these days; one is the independent miner and the other is the pool miner.

When mining first began, anyone could do it on their computer and the CPUs could handle the calculations. Back then, hash rates were in the region of kilohashes per second and the CPUs could handle that even if they did get hot and needed extra cooling. But then, as more miners got into the mix, you guessed it, the difficulty went up and so miners competed to increasing their hash power and so they started using their GPU cards which were significantly more powerful than the CPUs.

The competition become increasingly fierce and so specialized rigs were developed. These rigs could actually do little else. Companies like NVidia, manufacturers of video cards, started targeting this market instead of their usual gaming market, and they started offering more powerful hashing cards. Eventually, that gave way to specialized hashing machines called ASICs. These hashing machines couldn't do anything else except calculate millions of hashes.

When that didn't stop the competition, people started grouping their computers and buying up more hash power to coin, and then try to solve the puzzles that way, but that soon was outstripped as well.

Today, what you find are either large mining farms that have anywhere from 20 ASICS running 24 hours, or factories running hundreds of ASICs, or, on the other hand, you find people just buying the equipment and hooking on to mining pools.

Mining pools are just individual miners that get together and combine their smaller hashing power to become a large pool and become competitive in being able to solve the nonce puzzle.

Once the mining is complete and the hash complies with the constraint, that nonce is then left in the block and the hash is advertised. That hash is then used for the subsequent block and then that block is mined.

By doing it in this way, value moves from the physical world where work is done, to the online world where the coins are transacted. The miners spend considerable fixed and variable costs to mine the blocks and then allow the blocks to be verified, confirmed and added to the earlier block.

Chapter 5: Downside of Blockchain

There are numerous benefits to the blockchain technology and there are numerous uses to it in the form of coin, token and currency among other things. The thing about blockchains is that they are hard to grasp, and the maths behind them tends to make people cringe when they are first introduced to it.

Then you add that to the fact that the programming behind the blockchain can be complex when you get down to the nitty-gritty of it, but my advice to you is to not let it distort your perception of the next new thing in finance.

The system's complexity varies based on who you ask. For me, the system is as simple as it can be. For a recent computer grad, there could be some conceptual challenges, but the guys who are in their mid-careers are the ones that will find it a little strange as it is a completely new paradigm. Don't worry though, as it just takes a little getting used to.

When it comes to transaction costs, it is mostly cost-efficient but, for those of you who think that Bitcoin is absolutely free, you need to think again. There are costs associated with it, but the benefits far outweigh those costs – unless you are trying to make micro payments and then the cost is not worth it if you are on the Bitcoin platform. For that, you should try one of the other new coins.

The biggest downside is that it is facing a steep uphill battle with lawmakers in countries that are advanced in technology and backward in thinking. Countries are used to keeping track on their citizens for one reason or another, and their knee-jerk reaction to Bitcoin has been severe. Tread carefully and be nimble when it comes to investing. Check with your lawyer if you have to, but even if you do not agree with the law, you have to follow it.

Conclusion

Cryptocurrencies are made possible by the distributed ledger that is kept honest by an independent system called the blockchain. The idea of the blockchain is to harness the power of the crowd to automatically verify and remember. These nodes are central to the blockchain network and provide a valuable service.

As far as the blockchain is concerned, it is in its infancy. There is a long way to go before you start to see the real power of the blockchain, but if the start is any indication, it will be safe to say that the short-term benefits of using the blockchain in a lot of other distributed technologies would be extremely beneficial.

Cryptocurrency has got a bad rap from those who do not understand it and those who are threatened by it – be that threat real or perceived. They like to throw Bitcoin and the blockchain into the category of criminal activity. I don't buy that for one second. Privacy is the bedrock of our democracy, but that privacy has been eroded slowly in the name of security and where has that got us? Events like that of advanced psychographic manipulation on social media, and even large scale monitoring by the powers that be.

The blockchain has become the core of a number of diverse technologies; even companies such as IBM have started to dive into it in a big way. Cloud storage companies are looking at blockchain technologies to be able to perfect distributed storage that is virtually impossible to destroy or hack.

Take, for instance, a company that is combining the utility of distributed file storage and the versatility of cryptocurrency and creating a token out of it. I am only bringing that up here because I want to show you how diverse blockchains can be.

The way this works is that the blockchain is created by nodes in the system and all the nodes in the system contribute a percentage of their hard drive to the network. In turn, what they do is store some of their contents on the network that is kept track of by a blockchain. The blockchain charges those who store data and then takes that data, encrypts it, and breaks it up into small fragments and scatters it across the network. When a user wants to retrieve it, he just has to enter his private key and he gets access to all his data that is brought back to him using BitTorrent technology for downloads.

Those who want to use this service purchase a cryptocurrency or token (like Bitcoin) and then pay that token on a periodic basis for the service to store the data. The person providing the hard-drive space gets a portion of income each time his drive space is used. The person using it automatically depletes his coin reserve as it goes to the administrator of the blockchain and the nodes that are storing the data.

The income for the nodes is almost automatic and on autopilot. They just need to keep their computer on and, as time goes by, the coin that is paid for the storage accumulates over time.

The point of this example is two-fold. The first, to exhibit the flexibility and nature of blockchains, and the second, to introduce the next wave of distributed apps that will be built on blockchains and parallel the token and coin market.

The larger the coin and token market expand, the more that results in the advance of Bitcoin. It somehow seems that the entry point for a number of the cryptocurrencies is the Bitcoin; and the exchange for these tokens and coins has become quite vibrant, and do not show any signs of slowing down.

Your interest in the blockchain and the coin above it, is one probably driven by smart intuition and should be promoted. You should advance your interest in this because it is the start of a new paradigm in commerce and finance.

There are a few other areas that you should look into if you want to take this business seriously. There are issues in cryptocurrency mining that you may want to advance. There is a huge industry out there that is in its nascent stages. On the other hand, if you are more the trading type and are not to savvy with the technical aspects of things, then maybe cryptocurrency trading could be something that you could get into. Bitcoin trading has tremendous potential because it is a volatile market and program traders love to trade with volatile markets because there are profits to be made in either direction and there is a large amount of arbitrage opportunity as well.

If mining and trading is not your thing, but you are in other areas of technology, you can also think of the ICO option ICOs are Initial Coin Offerings and they are ways to raise capital by issuing crypto-assets.

There are numerous areas that you can get into to take up the opportunity that is present in this vast, new field of cryptocurrencies. You did the absolute right thing by starting with this book to get an idea of the blockchain technology that sits under the crypto-asset that rides on top.

Blockchains will revolutionize the Internet and change the face of it. The signs are already afoot, and what remains are the passage of time and the flow of ideas. The larger institutional edifices are starting to crumble in the face of the blockchain technology and the implementation of it will be nothing short of revolutionary. The movement from centralized architectures to decentralized ones will be in full force within the end of this century, and it will form the backbone of the internet of things. It will also serve as the preferred route of deployment for Artificial Intelligence and, together, AI, blockchains and the Internet of Things will be the way of the future.

Welcome to a new world.

Links and References

https://bitnodes.earn.com/

https://passwordsgenerator.net/sha256-hash-generator/

https://blockchain.info/

https://www.random.org/strings/

https://bitcoin.org/en/download

https://charts.bitcoin.com/chart/price#cat-market

https://blockchain.info/charts/difficulty

https://blockchain.info/charts/hash-rate

https://bitinfocharts.com/comparison/bitcoin-confirmationtime.html